The Principles and Practices of *Universal* Enhancement

The Principles and Practices of *Universal* Enhancement

Volume Four:
Venturing Beyond the Iron Gate

by Thomas E. Pomeranz, Ed.D.

Edited by Virginia Vath

High Tide Press
Homewood, Illinois

A HIGH TIDE BOOK
Published by High Tide Press Inc.
3650 West 183rd Street, Homewood, Illinois 60430
www.hightidepress.com / toll-free: 1-800-698-3979

Pomeranz, Thomas E. The principles and practices of Universal
Enhancement / by Thomas E. Pomeranz, Ed.D.
Volume 4. First ed.

ISBN 1-892696-18-5

Edited by Virginia Vath
Cover illustration by Rob Colvin
Cover and book design by Diane J. Bell

Printed in the United States of America

First Edition

Printed on acid-free paper. ∞

To my wife, Diane–my partner, inspiration and chief of the UE Police.

Table of Contents

Introduction

Universal Enhancement is not a new invention; it is, rather, a discovery. It is a key to unlock and open the closed doors that have served as barriers to countless persons who have been shut out of the world most individuals take for granted. It is the key to a world in which all people are allowed to have a life. It is a magic key in that its use requires not only using the right words, but also the motivation to do things differently. This book can be used as a key, but it is only a tool. You will have to bring your own resources to bear, as you use this tool to help people unlock new opportunities for themselves and their communities.

The notion that some people have been "cast out" from the main-

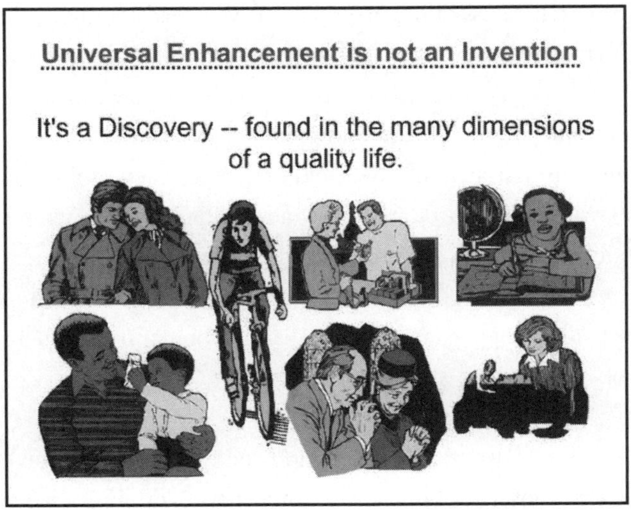

stream of society will be used as the central metaphor. They are Outsiders. The primary examples of the phenomenon of being cast out are those persons who, because of diminished cognitive and adaptive abilities, are considered to have mental retardation or intellectual disabilities.

Universal Enhancement is "universal" because it applies equally to all conditions that have been used as the basis for excluding people from full participation in their own lives. The tools of Universal Enhancement are applicable to all of us, regardless of ability or disability, as we seek to "enhance" the quality of our lives. "Having a life" is a challenge we all face in some form. We all have our demons.

One reason intellectual disabilities is used as the primary exemplar is that the provision of services and supports for people with intellectual disabilities is the field in which I have had the most experience. Unfortunately, the other reason people with intellectual disabilities can serve as examples is that, for the most part, their lives have been stolen from them by the combined forces of ignorance, prejudice and fear.

Someone who works or lives with people who have mental illness, however, would see the opportunities of Universal Enhancement through the lens of that experience. The same holds true for people more familiar with the isolating and deprecating effects of being elderly or having no parents or being an unwed mother. The principles hold true, regardless of the exemplar. As you read through the book, you can mentally substitute the life circumstances with which you are most familiar or concerned (perhaps a challenge you yourself experience) for the one used as an example.

The main narrative of this book, the text of each of the chapters, can be read straight through. It provides all the history, principles and strategies you need for understanding Universal Enhancement. Scattered throughout this narrative are the following sub-sections that can be read or skipped, according to your particular need and interest:

Tales

Tales are illustrative stories, poems and collective conversation culled from the author's 30-plus years of clinical and administrative experience. These stories demonstrate the principles of Universal Enhancement and present concrete visions of how those principles change peoples' lives.

Toolboxes

Toolbox sections are practical techniques and procedures you can use as you implement the principles of Universal Enhancement. They will demonstrate innovative and effective ways of behaving. The checklist and program suggestions on Toolbox pages may be used in your work or efforts to assist others in enhancing the quality of their life.

Maxims

Maxims are short, succinct phrases that encapsulate the tools and approaches of Universal Enhancement. They will form the core of this new approach and will prompt and inspire your new behavior. If your friends, neighbors and coworkers learn the Maxims, you will share a new vocabulary, a short-hand communication device you can use to remind each other of what you are trying to do and where you are trying to go. The author claims no exclusive rights to the ideas contained in this book, because they are ideas found lying about in everyone's lives. They have been gathered and given form, but they came from everyone and thus belong to everyone. They are truly universal.

It is my hope that as you read what is compiled here, you will experience the same kind of "Aha!" feeling I have had as my new perceptions took shape. You might find yourself thinking, "These ideas are so simple; why didn't we think of and use them much earlier?"

The answer lies in our deeply rooted perception of people we see as being radically different from ourselves. This ability to see some groups of people as wholly "other" than ourselves has, historically, allowed us to act in ways we may later find incomprehensible.

Upon touring the Holocaust Museum in Washington, D.C., a young man asked his father, "How could we have done these things to them?" And the father answered, "The first step was using the word 'them.' After that the rest was easy."

This book is the result of many thousands of hours spent working in the field of services for people with disabilities. I must express my deep appreciation to countless teachers, coworkers, and friends, as well as to the people I have served and supported who have helped shape the principles of Universal Enhancement. I hope this book will bring us all more such relationships, more opportunities to learn, to exchange ideas, and to affect the lives of people.

The Principles and Practices of *Universal* Enhancement

1

Beyond Mere Integration to Full Inclusion

The guiding principle, which is the essence of the notion of Universal Enhancement, is inclusion.

We have strolled through a brief history of the ways human service workers, family and friends have tried to provide support, care, and opportunities to people whose life conditions have cast them as Outsiders.

In Volume One, the Medical/Custodial Model was analyzed with its "do for" approach, concerned mostly with providing a safe, isolated, sterile environment for people who were seen as being medically defective.

The advent of the Developmental Model in Volume Two was reviewed as a better way, which sought to help people with developmental disabilities progress through the steps of normal child development.

The evolution of the Habilitation Model, also in Volume Two, was traced, noting that this approach was motivated, in part, by the regulations of the Intermediate Care Facility-Mental Retardation program. With its annual plans, this federal program was designed to help people acquire the skills they were thought to need before moving to a less restrictive environment.

The next stage, Universal Enhancement, is herein defined as a vision of a possible future, a paradigm shift that is affecting how services are funded, organized and provided. The strategies of Universal

Enhancement go to the heart of how people live their lives. Universal Enhancement is a rising tide that has already changed the lives of many individuals, but it is, unfortunately, only a distant rumble to many more.

A Paradigm Shift

In the preceding volumes, much of the groundwork was laid for the paradigm shift of Universal Enhancement. It was necessary to examine the language we use, the definitions that influence our perception of disabilities and handicaps, our understanding of the role of helpers, the use of time, where work should take place, and the values that inform the decisions we make. All of these influences–definitions, language, perceptions, and values–are affected by a paradigm shift. Universal Enhancement, being such a paradigm shift, alters both our awareness of ourselves and our approach to those who have been cast as Outsiders.

What is sought is not merely "rearranging the chairs on the deck of the Titanic," but urging that a new ship be built. Universal Enhancement is the vehicle that provides the systems and tools required for the building of that new ship, for the realization of the glorious future desired for and by people who have been treated as Outsiders.

These tools are uncomplicated and easy to apply. Most importantly, they are free. There is no catalogue in which to purchase them. Their use will not violate current regulations and standards under which we operate. The use of the tools does not require anyone's permission for their implementation. They are culture free and location free. Universal Enhancement is the means we use to get and maintain a life for ourselves. Thus, implementation of the tools will come naturally for many.

Universal Enhancement

It is time now to elaborate on just what is meant by this mysterious term Universal Enhancement. By analyzing its parts, we extend our understanding of the ways in which Universal Enhancement gives form to enhancing one's quality of life. Universal means all-embracing, all-reaching, "not limited or restricted." Enhancement is defined as "to raise, make greater, improve in quality or condition."[1] Putting the words together, we see Universal Enhancement as an increase in the quality of life of all people, without restrictions or limits, regardless of ability or disability.

That seems like a tall order, and so it is. Paradigm shifts always deliver tall orders; they demand that a stretch be made. Nothing less than this will bring us the world in which all individuals are treated as equals, free from institutional oppression, emancipated. Moving with the flow of Universal Enhancement will require nothing less than a conversion experience–an epiphany–in people who are invested in the old ways of doing and speaking. Though the changes will be painful for some, I have great hope that those changes are possible.

Those of us who have lived with the old way of treating people, who have been part of the dehumanization of institutionalized lives, are the most excited about doing things differently. We should be unabashed in our celebration of this new paradigm, and not ashamed to proselytize.

It will take a great deal of effort and zeal to promote the concepts of Universal Enhancement to the "nonbelievers." The results gained in using these concepts will only serve to enhance the lives of those we support. The quantitative and qualitative advantages will be significant. One of the most prevalent claims advanced by Universal Enhancement is that it can help resolve many of the problems that have resulted when we attempted to impose the various other theoretical models on individuals.

In the same manner that elements of religious belief are proven through their "fruits," it must be proven that Universal Enhancement tools are potent and true because they bear fruit in the form of better lives for all people. The impact of Universal Enhancement can

1 Webster's New World Dictionary (New York: Prentice Hall / Macmillan, 1994), 451.

be seen daily in the lives of many people–those we have the good fortune to serve and those with whom it is our pleasure to share the work of supporting in this field.

A Model of Inclusion

Though Universal Enhancement transcends all models, there is a model in current use that most closely embodies the vision of Universal Enhancement. This model has gained some currency in the human service field, as a result of court orders and empowerment movements that have served to dismantle the old institutional models. This movement is called inclusion. There are three steps that form the cornerstones of this model. They are integration, participation, and relationships.

Integration

We usually think of segregation as an injustice perpetrated against a minority, who are excluded from the opportunities afforded those who are in the majority mainstream, and so it is. Segregation means separation–people living in separate worlds, with separate standards and separate goals. It means living on the reservation, in the ghetto, in the institution.

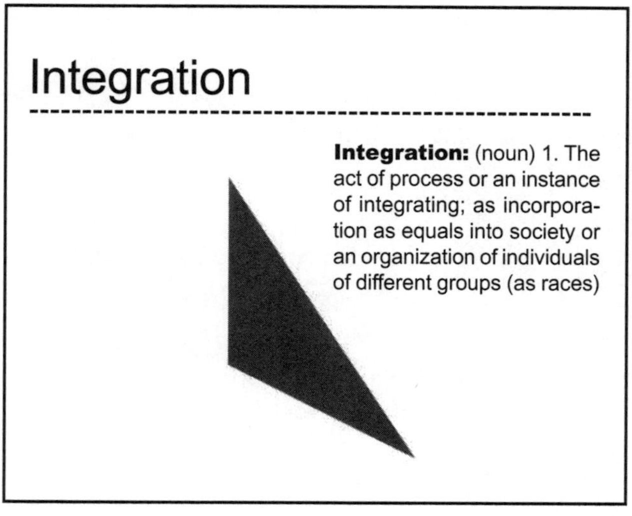

In American history, we are most familiar with the word segregation as it applied to the separation of people on the basis of race. As a nation, we challenged the acceptability of such separation in the historic *Brown v. Board of Education of Topeka, Kansas*, ruling by the Supreme Court in 1954. In that decision, taking the position that separate is inherently unequal, Chief Justice Earl Warren wrote:

> To separate [Negro children] from others of similar age and qualifications solely because of their race generates a feeling of inferiority as to their status in the community that may affect their hearts and minds in a way unlikely ever to be undone.... We conclude that in the field of public education the doctrine of "separate but equal" has no place. Separate educational facilities are inherently unequal.[2]

It was 20 years before the same principle was applied to children who had disabilities (PL 94-142, The Right to Education of All Handicapped Children Act of 1975), and even today, mainstreaming is not as common in public schools as it ought to be. Children with disabilities are still educated in separate, self-contained classrooms, often in separate, special schools. Indeed, in the context of how we have separated individuals with disabilities from the mainstream of society, *special* is often a code word for separate, as in Special Olympics or Special Education.

There is more to segregation, though, than the diminution of opportunities for the Outsiders who are victims of segregation. Segregation of people into separate groups denies the majority the opportunity of knowing people in those other groups. This "not knowing" (the literal meaning of ignorance) creates prejudice, a judgment occurring prior to knowing. And prejudice allows people to be judged on the basis of what we think we know about them (judging the contents by the label), rather than on our relationships with real, individual people.

I had a friend who grew up in a suburb of Chicago, which, as late

[2] *Brown v. Board of Education of Topeka, Kansas*, 74 Sup. Ct. 686 (1954)

as 1965, had all white residents. The high school of 2,500 students was all white. The Boy Scout troop was all white. The church was all white. There were no laws against people of other racial and ethnic groups being there. It was de facto segregation. How many relationships do you think my friend had with African-American people or people of Hispanic or Asian background? Of course, none. And in communities where black people or Buddhist people or people with disabilities live only with "their own kind," no one has a chance to learn from each other. When he started college in New York and his roommate was Jewish, think of what he learned from his roommate's family and they from him.

One of the first characteristics of an institution reviewed in Volume One was that it kept people remote from the mainstream of society, isolated from opportunities for learning and relationships. People with disabilities were believed to have an entirely different set of needs from the rest of us who lived in the homes and apartments in the cities and towns of this country. In order to meet their special needs (carefully avoiding any reference to society's need not to have to see and interact with them), people with disabilities were put into facilities designed to care for them. They were placed there. The same thing was done with Native Americans, under the guise of their own protection. Our elders are often placed, supposedly for their own good.

MAXIM: *Being a priority on a placement list is not seeing the light at the end of the tunnel. It is standing on the edge of a precipice.*

Such placement usually deprives people of opportunities, but not only for those who are moved away. The policy of segregation on the basis of difference (competence, skin color, or cultural background) also deprives the people who remain behind. Normatives, the people who live in communities sanitized of anyone who is too different from the norm, are denied the opportunity of knowing and interacting with many people who possess charm, humor, and their own quirky wisdom.

Robert Perske, in his wonderful 1980 book *New Life in the Neighborhood*, wrote about the advent of community placements such as group homes: "Neighborhoods will discover that there are not enough of these citizens with handicaps to go around. Some neighborhoods will have to go without!"[3]

Participation

Integration of people typically treated as Outsiders is an exciting and necessary first step. When group homes first began opening in towns and neighborhoods, and people began to move out of large, centralized facilities into these new places, many people believed they had it made at last.

There was excitement about people who were deinstitutionalized. They could now attend a neighborhood church, rather than just going to the chapel on the institution campus. Integration had been achieved and it was believed that was what it was all about. It was assumed integration was the desired outcome. But we were shortsighted. We were limited by a vision that did not encompass the dreams and desires of the people we sought to serve.

The new paradigm shift of Universal Enhancement forces one to ask deeper, more complex questions than simply whether or not the people we are serving and supporting have achieved integration. The more relevant inquiry is, "What are they doing when they're there, in the integrated setting?"

Yes, there were men and women going to the neighborhood movie theater, but our excitement blinded us to what often was happening. Staff were taking them.

Well, what's wrong with that?

What's wrong is that integration, in and of itself, does little to improve the quality of people's lives. It often fails to deal with many of the challenging kinds of behavior that are learned in institutional set-

3 Robert and Martha Perske, *New Life in the Neighborhood* (Nashville, TN: Abingdon Press, 1980) 30.

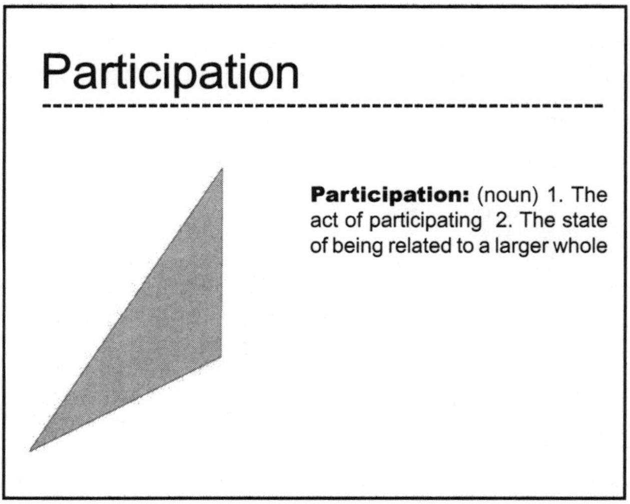

tings. And, it doesn't do much to help people grow, develop, and become more independent because it lacks an essential element of a quality life.

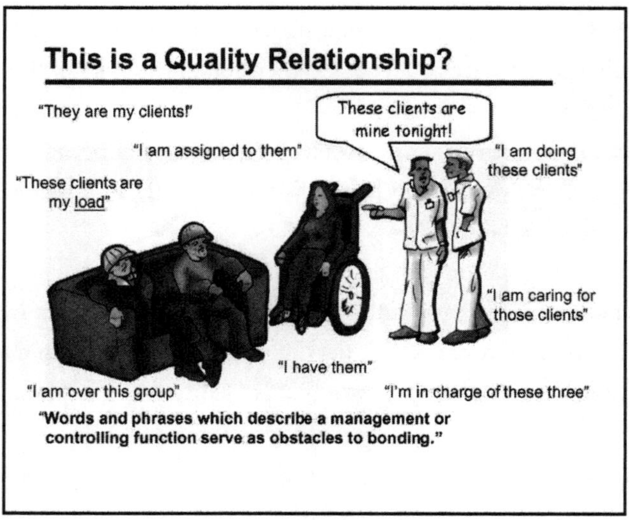

Participation–affecting your environment

To measure the degree of participation in an activity, we must ask, In what ways is that person involved in that activity? Several issues arise around participation in a trip to the movie theater. Will the man or woman going to the movies be allowed the opportunity to carry the money and buy the movie ticket, or will the staff carry the money and buy the ticket? Who will choose which movie to go to? Who will hand the ticket to the ticket taker? Who will keep the ticket stub? Who will decide where to sit? Who has the option to decide it's not a very good movie and it's time to leave? Unless the answer is the person who is receiving support, integration has brought no significant improvement over the old institutional way.

Feeling that the above depiction paints a very unrealistic expectation for people with disabilities, you may respond with questions of your own: Won't some people always have to be taken to the movies? If the person is so physically limited that their arms are contracted and they can hardly move, or they can't see or can't speak, how can they buy a ticket or choose a movie?

The answer has been previously given: We're going to take what we can get closest to what we (they) want. A person may need almost total

Being Missed

Having relationships - and being part of your community means being missed by others when absent .

assistance, but as I offer the assistance needed, I'm going to think out loud, "Now, Bryan, we're going to get the ticket. We need that five dollars you placed in your billfold before we left." And even if he attempts to put the money in his mouth, that is not a justification for denying Bryan the opportunity to remove the bills from his wallet, even though he may require a lot of support in doing so. The individual's limitation, his lack of skill, is not a sanction for us to do for, but a mandate to assist. As Bryan's assistant, I become his agent, working on his behalf, remaining silent and in the background until summoned by the occasion of his need for me. As a support staff we must be quiet voices in the background. We must remain transparent, for it is their life.

Continuing with the example of the trip to the movie theater, Bryan may need me to assist him in getting his money out of his pocket or wallet and presenting it at the ticket window. If Bryan is unable to reach the window, I may have to assist him further, but I will still ask, acting as his agent, "Which movie do you want to see, 'Space Bimbos' or 'Godzilla Goes Hawaiian'?"

He makes no apparent response, but I know Bryan likes loud monster films, so I say, "Oh, Godzilla. Okay, one ticket for Godzilla."

I may have to assist in getting the ticket from the window by placing

Seeing the Individual

Can you identify these traits in the persons for whom you provide support?

- **Compassion** **Gregarious** **Honest** **Independent**
- **Integrity** **Fidelity** **Kind** **Optimistic**
- **Sincere** **Industrious** **Sensitive** **Cautious**
- **Assertive** **Forgiving** **Shy** **Patient**
- **Empathetic** **Determined** **Spontaneous** **Principled**
- **Creative** **Motivated** **Generous**

We must be able to see through the individual's disabilities and challenges and appreciate the beauty of their personality.

it in Bryan's hand or on his lap or in his pocket. "Bryan, here's your ticket. You'll need to give it to the ticket taker when we get inside the door."

Now I may have to assist Bryan in pushing his wheelchair through the door. "These doors are hard to open when you use a wheelchair." All the while, Bryan appears not to be responding to anything in his environment, but he is actually doing quite a lot. He is listening to me as I think out loud, and his acceptance of my extensive assistance may be, at this time, the fullest extent to which he can participate. The important point is that I am *doing with* Bryan, rather than *doing for* him.

The major difference between doing for and doing with is in our mind-set, in our way of thinking about what we're doing. It is an attitude, if you will. In utilizing the tools of Universal Enhancement, I must think of myself as going to the movies with Bryan, rather than taking him to the movies. It is this approach that makes all the difference.

If I adopt the *do with* mind-set, I must acknowledge and respect the fact that it is Bryan's money and Bryan's ticket and Bryan's refreshments and Bryan's place to sit. When I arrive at this realization, I am positioned to act as the support and assistant that I need to be. I will know my place and my function, which is to give Bryan the support he needs in order to enjoy his Saturday afternoon at the movies. This is participation–when a person is assisted in doing what he or she wants to do, not toted around like a doll or a pet, nor towed like a boat.

There is an edifying scene in the movie "Scent of a Woman." The young student, who has been hired to assist the retired colonel who is blind, takes hold of the colonel's arm to try to lead him through the doors at the airport. The colonel snaps at the student, "Are you blind?!"

The student, dumfounded, doesn't know what to say.

The colonel barks again, "I said, 'Are you blind?'"

The student answers sheepishly, "No."

"Then don't grab my arm," replies the Colonel. "I grab your arm."[4]

It seems almost petty, but the difference is crucial. Applying the

4 *Scent of a Woman*, prod. and dir. Martin Brest (Universal City, CA: MCA / Universal Home Video, 1993) videocassette.

principles of Universal Enhancement to facilitate participation guarantees that the one receiving assistance is in charge. And being in charge, making decisions and choices about your life, is what gives that life meaning and dignity. If the assistant is in charge, the person who needs help is just an appendage, just an object to be scheduled, taken, fed, moved, and programmed.

If integration fails to lead to participation, the doors to a quality life will remain closed. Let us not, through default, create little institutions on every block, in which people with differences live out their lives unrelated to the Normatives who live around them and are consequently precluded from enriching the lives of their neighbors and neighborhoods.

It is also only through participation in life's activities that relationships can be developed. If we take Linda to the grocery store, clamp her hand firmly to the shopping cart, and direct her through the aisles as we do her shopping for her, what is gained? How is Linda's life enhanced? This is little better than sitting in the day room watching staff-selected soap operas. Only through interaction with the other shoppers, the produce manager, the checkout clerks, the baggers, does the shopping trip take on real value and meaning.

Does this sound familiar? Remember "interacting with media?"

When a level of meaningful participation is realized, the whole community serves as the media for learning and growing. We could have a whole training program that consists of nothing but spending the day walking around town, meeting new people, encountering novel situations, meeting whatever challenges might present themselves–in short, participating in our town's or city's or neighborhood's ongoing life.

MAXIM: *Getting* out *(of the institution) is easy; getting* in *(to the community) is hard.*

You see, getting out of the institution is the easy part. Getting in to the community is much, much harder–for the community must be built.

TALE

Helen and the Bell Choir

There was a woman I met with who lived in a large metropolitan area on the East Coast. She was only three feet long, lying down. And lying down was where she was all the time. Her body was so contracted that she spent her day supported by a padded plywood board, maintained in position with Velcro straps. Due to a condition diagnosed as similar to anencephaly ("no brain"), she lacked vision and hearing. She was 44 years old, qualified to be considered an adult. But, the staff at the institution where she lived had given her a baby rattle so that she would "have something to do." Her name was Helen.

Helen moved out of the institution into a "home" with several other women. Despite her apparent disabilities, the staff in the home bonded with her. One of the staff (that we'll call Sue) got the novel idea of going to church with Helen.

As Helen didn't do much, she did not make many demands on the people who were with her. She didn't make any noises or engage in any behavior that would cause a disturbance. So Helen and Sue attended church together uneventfully.

A number of people who had very limited physical and cognitive abilities lived in Helen's home. Extensive occupational therapy services were provided to all of them, including Helen. The occupational therapist directed the staff to assist Helen in the use of a rolling pin. They would roll it back and forth to increase Helen's range of motion and palmar grasp–a functional outcome. But rolling a rolling pin back and forth when there's no dough to be rolled is not a meaningful activity. It is an activity completely lacking in one essential element that is required to turn engagement into valued learning opportunities. Sue tried to think of a more meaningful way for Helen to work toward increasing her range of motion and improving her palmar grasp.

The church the women attended had a wonderful bell choir. Sue could see by her facial expression that Helen could sense the vibration of the bells when they were played. Sue approached the director of the bell choir and asked if it would be possible for Helen to participate. The director must have thought Sue was joking. Here was a woman supported by a padded plywood board, with no vision and no hearing, no palmar grasp, unable to assist herself in any way, and this staff person wanted her to play in the bell choir!

The director finally agreed that Helen could attend some rehearsals.

She would be attached to the cart that provided her mobility, and Sue would be sitting next to her. In order to simplify the task for Helen, Sue asked the director if she could play one of the lower tone bells, one that was not played as often as others. Sue offered assistance and support by placing the bell in Helen's hand and moving her hand when it was Helen's time to ring the bell.

Each ringer in a bell choir is required to sit in the same place each time so that the bells are always in the same order. An older woman named Betty occupied the position next to Helen. At first, she felt a little uneasy about the situation. Betty was anxious about having to sit next to a little woman strapped to a padded plywood board. Helen is not the kind of person who usually comes to mind for the development of social relationships in a church bell choir. But Betty gradually overcame her discomfort in Helen's presence as Sue persisted in being very friendly on Helen's behalf.

Sue and Betty began talking on Sundays, though Betty never talked directly to Helen. Then one Sunday, as Sue was assisting Helen to ring her bell, Helen let out a laugh. This was very unusual for Helen, for no one had ever heard her make any kind of sound. Betty, sitting next to Helen as always, was struck by the humor and, without thinking, said, "Helen, did something tickle you?" Sue, on Helen's behalf, responded to Betty by saying, "Isn't that wonderful? Helen just laughed."

It broke the ice.

The next Sunday, when Helen came into the choir loft, Betty said, "Good morning, Helen. How are you doing this morning? Your dress really looks lovely. It's a nice day outside today, isn't it?" Betty had begun making casual conversation, just as all of us do when we're starting to get to know someone.

The chats continued for a few more Sundays. Betty began to develop a rapport with Helen. Betty is one of those people who understands intuitively what it means to think out loud and take what you can get closest to what you (they) want. She is a person who has water in her well.

One Saturday afternoon a few weeks later, Betty called the group home and asked for Sue. Betty was a little hesitant at first, beating around the bush as though there was something she wanted to say but didn't quite know how. Finally, she blurted out, "I don't know if this would be appropriate or not. I mean, I know you must have rules and things at that home. But I was wondering... do you think that tomorrow, after church, you and Helen could come over to my house for dinner?"

A connection had been made. A relationship had been formed. And that is what life is all about. That is inclusion.

Relationship

Inclusion is achieved through the social interactions that arise from participation in life's activities. Every relationship that you and I have entered into, excluding relationships with family members, has occurred because of our participation–our participation as an employee, our participation as a student, our participation as a volunteer, our participation in bowling leagues or hobby groups. Participation in life's activities is the source of relationships.

Participation is the key, which unlocks the opportunity for people to form and develop meaningful relationships. And meaningful relationships are the most important elements of almost everyone's vision

Relationship

Relationship

Relationship: (noun) 1. A connection, association, or involvement 2. An emotional or other connection between people

Keep 'em Dependent

Limiting opportunity, options, education and experience helps assure dependence

Oppressor	Oppressed
The chauvinistic husband	Abused wife
The white slave owner	Black slave
The loan shark	Debtor
The drug pusher	Drug addict
The pimp	Prostitute
The coal baron	Coal miner
	People with mental retardation

The oppressor has always known this about the oppressed

VALUED RELATIONSHIPS

How many relationships do the people you support have other than with:

- **Family members**
- **Paid relationships such as support staff, physician, dentist**
- **Individuals with disabilities with whom they work or live**

What is the relationship between an individual's competence and the number of valued relationships they have beyond those stated above?

What supports do you need to offer that will facilitate cognitively and physically challenged people in forming valued relationships?

Building Relationships

When was the last time you had "fun" with one of the persons whom you support?

Name a person you support whom you admire. Why do you admire them?

of quality of life. Relationships are what inclusion is all about. In fact, "relationships" could be a one-word definition of inclusion.

If you provide support for, are related to, or know of a person who has been segregated as an Outsider (as the result of a disability or other characteristic seen as socially unacceptable), ask yourself how many relationships that person has with people who are not immediate family members. How many of the relationships involve a person who is not paid to provide support services? How many involve someone who is not also a member of the same Outsiders group? The answer, too often, is zero. In those instances where the individual has four or five relationships, it is likely that the person in question demonstrates considerable competence (is able to slip past the Gatekeepers). This shouldn't surprise us. How are people supposed to develop meaningful, life-enhancing relationships if they only have opportunities to spend time with family, support workers and others of their kind? How much meaning would your life have if your valued relationships were few or restricted?

Toolbox

Taking Stock

A good way to assess the quality of relationships in a group with which you work is to ask everyone to think of one person they know who has been excluded because of some personal characteristic. Then ask them the question mentioned above: How many relationships does that person have with people who are not paid to support him/her, are not members of his/her family, and are not also excluded due to the same life circumstance?

Ask the group to raise their hands, with fingers extended to show the number of relationships they came up with. A closed fist equals 0 relationships, one finger is 1, two fingers for 2, etc. Have the participants look all around the room at the raised hands. Ask the par-

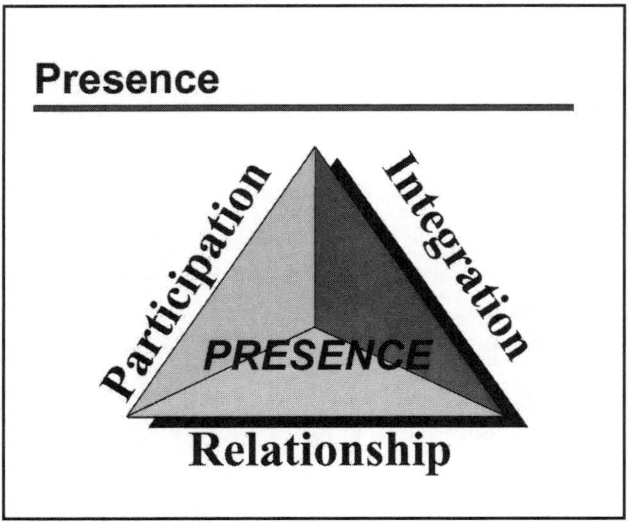

ticipants to take stock of the closed fists versus the hands with fingers.

It is always a chilling experience to see the forest of raised fists.

Next, ask the group to think about the cases where several fingers are raised. You can almost guarantee that the person represented by raised fingers has more competence than the person represented by a fist. The more challenging the person's disability, the fewer relationships that person is likely to experience.

Relationships are the key to the enrichment of people's lives, not just of people with Outsider status, but of all people. In order to achieve a high quality of life, all three elements of our quality of life triangle need to be present–integration, participation and relationship. When all elements are built upon, then the person who is newly returned to our communities from exile in the land of Outsiders will be able to establish a presence, and will finally have a life and be somebody.

2

The Elements of Getting a Life

Some of the tools used to facilitate and support inclusion for all people were discussed in preceding chapters. Techniques of Inclusion such as *Take what you can get closest to what you (they) want* and *Don't do anything alone* are part of the process of helping people grow, develop, and become more independent. As people become more integrated into the mainstream of their communities, they have more opportunities to participate in the ongoing activities of community life. Participation then leads to the relationships, which foster inclusion.

Anyone who has used the "training" techniques that are the legacy from the Habilitative Model years must sense immediately that such techniques as backward chaining and strict command structures are very different from the *do with* activities proposed. Training techniques of the old type are part of the *do to* mentality, the old paradigm. They are remnants of the habilitation principle that people need to learn new skills in order to move into a less restrictive environment (in order to have an increased range of options in their life). As stated earlier, we need to advocate that everybody is ready for everything, right now.

Going beyond mere training to encompass the concept of support, an almost limitless set of opportunities and possibilities is generated. We don't have to wait until people learn to be more independent, if we are willing to support and encourage full inclusion in all activities of society and community. Indeed, interdependence, relying on a network of friends and coworkers and neighbors for assistance as needed, is the way most of us Normatives live our lives. Why should it be any different for people whose needs for support are of a different type or more extensive than our own?

It isn't any different. That is the central judgment and precept of Universal Enhancement. Whether this judgment is based on some variation of the Golden Rule (Do unto others as you would have them do unto you); or stems from a theological belief that all human beings are children of God; or comes from the purely pragmatic and introspective understanding that our lives are enriched by being open to relationships with all kinds of people, the outcome is the same. No person is completely alien to us, so different that his or her needs and desires are incomprehensible and strange to us.

When the challenge is accepted to tear down the barriers that separate us from other people, we immediately know what to do when we advocate for Outsiders, because we know what we need in order to live lives of completion and satisfaction. You do not need university degrees or clinical experience to begin the process of Universal Enhancement. All you need is an open mind and a willing heart. If we are motivated and enthusiastic to support people in realizing the possibilities and potentials of their lives, it should be easy to find ways to become valued co-contributors in all the relationships we form with people who have been seen as Outsiders. The tools that follow are merely guidelines, some directions in which to place our focus as we all work together to achieve Universal Enhancement.

Supporting Inclusionary Behavior

Inclusion does not happen overnight, with the waving of advocacy's magic wand. The road to inclusion is often a long one, with hills to climb and sharp bends to negotiate. The vision of Universal Enhancement would be nothing but a map of fantasyland if it did not offer a vehicle for helping people move from Outsider status to inclusion. The tools of Universal Enhancement will help you help others to get past the Gatekeepers and other obstacles that barricade the road.

The process of providing supports is not amorphous. The process of Universal Enhancement is a logical structure in which we provide support. It provides the opportunities to participate in a natural flow of life or in basic routines, often referred to as positive rituals. It presents opportunities for individuals to truly become part of life enhancement experiences. When people come from places where they are not valued, where they have not been provided the opportunity to participate in life's positive rituals, there is an acclimation process. The way we relate to individuals to support inclusion into a new life is multi-layered. It will take a variety of supports for individuals who have not had experience with the routines of life to become integrated into a life where we can support the development of relationships. In essence, we need to teach people how to shed their Outsider status and overcome the obstacles that have been barriers to having a valued life.

Confronted with life in the real world, it is difficult to know where to start. Part of our role in the transition process is to lead individuals down the path where there are opportunities to experience the artifacts of life. One does not move instantly from a life of restricted or limited opportunity to one of enrichment. There is no magical wand to make the transition happen, even though it may seem like a magical process–an epiphany–to see an individual life evolve from one phase to the next where they are participants in a community.

We work under a *do with* model, in which we see ourselves as collaborators in the process of helping people realize their hopes, dreams and desires. Those of us who are paid for this work really do *work for* "clients" when we see ourselves in this way, in the sense that we are engaged to act in their behalf. This way of working truly puts the support recipient in the driver's seat, making choices, setting goals, and determining priorities.

The following processes can serve as stepping stones that help us support individuals who have been negatively affected by institutional characteristics:

- Mend
- Socialize

- Connect
- Communicate
- Initiate

Mend

The first step, mending, is necessary because many people come to us with something broken. Long years of institutional living may have broken their spirits or their wills. Their choice-making ability may be rusty with disuse. And, most importantly, the ties that bind people with one another in a community have been severed. A time of mending is needed.

This mending process used to be called stabilization, a term inherited from the Medical/Custodial Model, wherein the "patient" who cannot be cured can at least be "stabilized." Stabilization was seen as the best that could be hoped for people who were not deemed capable of having regular lives. The Medical/Custodial Model used admission as treatment. Once you were in the safe facility, your condition could be stabilized. Does that sound like a goal you or your loved ones have for your lives? Do you want your life to be stable? Probably not. You probably want your life to contain variety and change, adventure and challenge.

MEND

- Design Life Stiles.
    - Identify the obstacles in that person's life.
    - Modify the environment.
- Redirect and Protect.
    - Offer gentle physical support.
    - Support choice making.
- Consider a temporary medication plan.
    - Assess and review the need for medication.
    - Start low, go slow.

Design Universal Life Stiles

The former Outsider who is trying to be reintegrated into the ongoing life of his community faces formidable obstacles. Gatekeepers of various stripes, from fearful neighbors to skeptical employers, do their best to keep the barriers intact between the world of the Outsider and the protected world of Us. As we assist former Outsiders to get a life, several different approaches could be taken to tear down these barriers.

The methods of the radical advocate could be adopted in an attempt to smash the barriers, through protests and rights legislation. But that approach is liable to bring a backlash that would seriously limit the universal (for all people) element of what we are trying to do. Or we could teach Outsiders patience, expecting them to accept that many people are ignorant and scared and that they (the Outsiders) must wait apologetically until some Gatekeeper becomes enlightened enough to crack the gate enough for admission.

Still another approach is to face the barrier head-on and figure out a way over it. In rural areas, pastures are sometimes delimited with fences made of rock and stone. Instead of using gates (difficult to build into a rock wall), people use stiles, steps built over the wall that allow people to walk easily up and over the barrier. Life Stiles are not specifically designed for certain groups of individuals but apply to all people. A common bond we share is that barriers of one type or another challenge all of us. What makes us unique and individual is the approach we take to overcoming those barriers. But, our commonality is in confronting life's obstacles and overcoming them. When used as the means for overcoming obstacles in people's lives, these steps are called Life Stiles.

The first activity in building Life Stiles is identification of the barriers. What are the obstacles to this particular person's inclusion? That is, are we trying to step over a two-foot high wall of loose rocks that may require only a steadying hand to surmount? Or a five-foot wall that necessitates the building of several sturdy steps? Or are we trying to scale a ten-foot wall of finished stone that will require ropes, climbing gear, and a couple of pulleys?

It is important to note here that identifying barriers in a person's life is very different from identifying that person's deficits (the way we did under the Developmental and Habilitation models). Blaming a person for the wall before them, for the gate slammed in their face, will not help them get to the other side. What will help is the identification of an obstacle as a challenge that can be overcome through creativity and perseverance.

My friend Donald is just beginning a job at Hardee's. He has to complete many tasks, such as wiping tables, washing trays, emptying trash, filling condiment bottles, and cleaning the parking lot. He can't follow the typical task checklist, because he can't read. Now, we could identify his lack of reading ability as the obstacle and tell him he can have a job as soon as he learns to read. Or, we could design a life stile for overcoming the barrier–a picture card that helps Donald remember what tasks he needs to complete.

Life Stiles overcome barriers right now. There is no waiting for someone else to change (the myth of the enlightenment of Gatekeepers) or waiting until the Outsider acquires new skills (the myth of habilitation). The challenge is to identify the obstacle and to design some way of getting over it. We need to come up with ways of modify-

Barriers and attitudes cause handicaps, not disabilities.

ing the environment, rather than trying to modify the person who is challenged by obstructions. We must go beyond strengths and needs assessments that lead to training programs. Rather, we should develop assessments of obstacles that lead to lists of creative Life Stiles. If we get out our hammers and nails and help an Outsider build steps to get over walls, she and we will be walking in the neighboring field in no time.

The ever vigilant, astute reader asks, "But what do you do when confronted by someone who wants to take your head off or throw the TV set through the living room window? What kind of life stile do I build for him?"

Answering this concerned person by suggesting all she has to do is form relationships and encourage community inclusion would be naive. She is dealing with challenging behaviors that have arisen in response to the kinds of life circumstances that thwart the usual processes of socialization. The behaviors do not disintegrate or disappear overnight nor are they "cured" with Universal Enhancement. The primary purpose of Universal Enhancement is improving the quality of life for individuals. Introducing individuals to a world of Universal Enhancement often results in a secondary purpose of reducing challenging behavior.

A person is not going to get the supports he needs if everyone is afraid of him. He is not going to succeed in even the first step, that of integration, if his behavior is so threatening and damaging that community officials feel justified in locking him away in a nursing home or a juvenile detention center or a state psychiatric hospital.

Toolbox

The Three I's of Consequation

During a period of mending, we may need to apply particular consequences to behavior that is serving as a barrier to inclusion. In order for these consequences to truly be opportunities for learning, rather than punitive reactions, we can follow the Three I's. Consequences must be:

- Immediate: Responsive to the current event. Never threaten; never promise.
- Intense: Stronger than competing events and rewards.
- Impersonal: Directed at the behavior, not at the person.

Often the first thing we need to do in helping someone mend is to arrange a "prosthetic environment." Such an environment, responsive to the needs of a particular individual, immediately provides a situation that will give that person the best chance of beginning the process of mending. For example, we provide the wife who is abused with a shelter in which she can heal from her wounds and make a start at getting a new, safe life. Or we provide the person with alcoholism with a detox opportunity, a place where he is prevented from obtaining alcohol long enough to begin the process of recovery. Notice that these examples are actually a limiting of people's freedoms and opportunities. Such limitation is acceptable if it is only the first step in the process.

The provision of a temporary prosthetic environment is similar to

Environmental Restrictions

The restrictions and adaptations made to respond to the unique protective oversight needs of each individual serves to restrict the freedom and options of others in the environment.

Concern	*Institutional Restriction*
Leaves without supervision/permission	*Install door alarms*
Uses mops and broom handles as weapons	*Lock up items*
Shreds linens	*Lock up items*
Afflicts self injury with knifes	*Lock up items*
Flushes toilet paper rolls down toilet	*Lock up items*
Ingests caustic substances i.e.. cologne, detergent	*Lock up items*

Seek Creative Alternatives

the way we child-proof a house where a 2-year-old lives. Rather than fighting an hourly battle to get little Johnny to leave the valuable Ming vase alone, we just put it up in the closet, replacing it with a cheaper one from a discount store. When we stop having to replace the inexpensive vase, the Ming will come back to the display shelf. Similarly, in residential settings for people who have challenging behaviors, we adapt the environment to the needs of the individual.

MAXIM: *The least restrictive environment is determined by the individual with the most severe disability.*

Engineering a supportive environment is a process that differs from the process of environmental sterilization that goes on in institutional settings. The latter results in the least restrictive environment being determined by the individual with the most severe disability. But creating a supportive environment, also called individualized adaptation, is more like the procedure for supporting choice-making. Start off with a small set of options, and increase the range of options as the person demonstrates increased choice-making ability.

If a person's level of aggressive behavior is so intense that the changes needed to help her mend would impinge on all others with whom she lives, then she may need to live by herself for a while. The goal is to avoid posing challenges that are too difficult for a person to meet, or obstacles that set them up for failure. When the challenges are mediated by good environmental engineering (a form of Life Stile), the person is likely to be more successful in dealing with opportunities for successful inclusion.

An important principle here, when making environmental adaptations in the name of mending, is that we don't want to make any changes that remove the possibility of learning to adapt. We don't want to remove opportunities in the process of providing supports. This is a tricky and difficult challenge.

An elegant example of such "a difference that doesn't make a difference" is the installation of curtains that are attached to their sliding hooks by means of plastic snaps. If someone, in a property destroying rage, pulls the curtains down, they can be easily reattached. This is a much more creative response than the typical institutional reaction–no more curtains. By coming up with a creative solution to the problem of curtain ripping, we are developing a true prosthetic environment, not just a sterilized one. The challenge is to make sure a person has all the media he or she needs for developing a meaningful quality of life, while at the same time taking steps to assure everyone's safety.

Redirect and Protect

Sometimes people need to be stopped from harming themselves or others. We cannot stand by and watch someone bite pieces out of his arm or stand in the middle of a busy street. If we cannot talk a person into directing their energy and attention into a more appropriate behavior, we may have to lay hands on them and offer them gentle restraint. It is important, when we find ourselves using restraint, to understand that it is a form of support, no different in function from a wheelchair or a job coach. Stopping a person from hitting other people, using as little force as possible, and always with an attitude of respect and concern, allows the person to do something he needs to do but is unable to do on his own–stop hurting himself or others. Within the value orientation of Universal Enhancement, restraint is not used as punishment. It is not used as therapy or training. It is not an exercise in controlling power. Rather, restraint is applied out of empathy, out of a desire to assure that the person does not hurt himself or others. It is a support that is offered only so much as it is needed, only because the behavior being blocked would otherwise preclude the possibility of the person being able to realize his or her own dreams and goals. If life has no meaning, people will behave in a way to cause the lives of others to have no value or meaning.

Restraint is something *done with* someone, while encouraging him or her to do as much as they can themselves. It is never something *done to* someone, out of a sense that we have a right to control a person we see as less worthy or less powerful than ourselves.

One way to keep this distinction in mind is to remember the principle of redirection: never try to get a person to stop doing something; get him to do something else. Restraint is not a closed box of tight control. It is, rather, a way of directing a person toward an acceptable way of dealing with rage or frustration or fear. We must always leave one side of the "corral" open. Taht side must face the appropriate direction

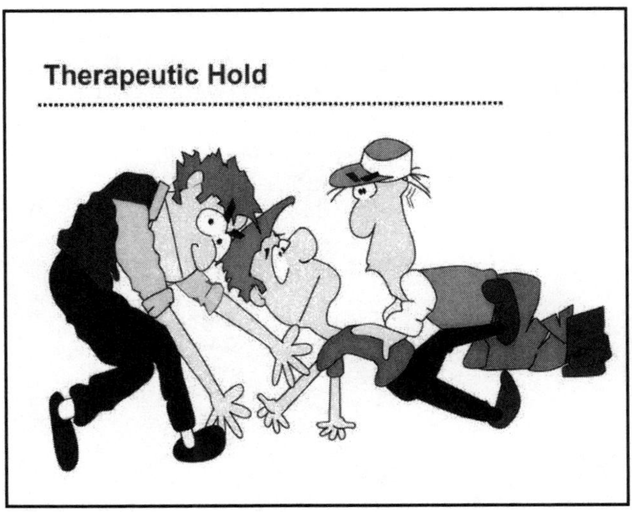

a person can take toward success.

Redirection is similar to the approach used in some gentle martial arts systems. The energy of attack and destruction is deflected in an alternative direction. Redirection leads the person to an increased ability to behave in ways that will increase their chances of acceptance and full inclusion.

It may seem strange, in a discussion of restraint and redirection, to bring up the topic of choice-making again. But having the ability to choose from among desirable options can be a key element of getting a life. Everyone wants to have some control over his or her own life. As seen in the discussion of institutional characteristics, such personal control is often taken away from the Outsider who is seen as not being able to control himself. A vicious, descending cycle is begun. The less opportunity for choice-making a person has, the more he is likely to try to control his environment in troubling and challenging ways. More external control is then laid on him, and the situation just gets worse. Instead of engaging in this counterproductive control cycle, it is best to offer meaningful, measured options as alternatives to violence and disruption. The three-sided corral model says, "Over here... This is where you can be successful. Which of these alternatives would you

Mechanical Restraint

like to try?" When people see a light at the end of the tunnel, they very often cease struggling to get off the track. It is crucial that we keep this vision in mind as we use prosthetic environments and the presentation of options as Life Stiles for the overcoming of obstacles.

Medication

Psychotropic medication should be seen in the same light as restraint. It is a support that may be needed by an individual to help him or her grow and develop. Medication should never be just an expedient solution that relieves us of the responsibility of supplying enough supports, enough staff assistance, enough environmental modification, enough opportunity to make choices. It should never be used to remove meaningful control over one's own life.

Medication should be seen, whenever possible, as a temporary intervention, like a crutch that is only needed until the broken leg heals, not as an essential part of "treatment."

Of course, there will be people who do not heal past their need for medication, despite our best efforts at helping them get a life. For these people, medication will be more like the prosthetic limb used by the person whose leg was amputated. It would be unreasonable to expect

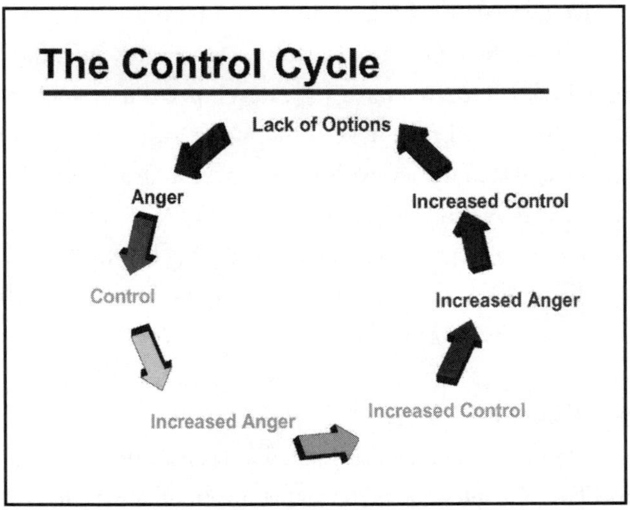

her to do without it.

Even for people who demonstrate a continued need for psychopharmaceutical support, we must always strive to help them use only as much support as is truly necessary in their particular circumstances. Medication must be used only with clear documentation of its effectiveness and at the lowest possible effective dose.

Mending is only the first step in supporting inclusion. Mending activities are most often necessary when people are trying to make the transition from institutional type settings to environments in which external controls are minimized. Mending is sometimes necessary because a former Outsider's reputation has been tarnished, and the staff or other people in his life are afraid. If everyone around a person is in fear of him, he will not have much opportunity to get on with his life.

Mending is often the most difficult and challenging task of inclusion; but when approached with an attitude of respect and support, it can be the step that brings the most immediate benefit to the person who has lived for years under the burdens of institutional systems.

Socialize

Another process that is often made necessary by the experience of having lived under the burden of institutional characteristics is socialization. Many people who have lived in environments over which they have had little control, or in circumstances in which they were treated with disrespect or abuse, have developed self-protective styles of relating to a world they have come to see as hazardous. It is not unusual to hear staff who provide supports for such an individual say, "He likes to be by himself" or "I can't get her to do things with the others." These caring staff people are confronted with the challenge of helping someone come out of a shell that has served him well, perhaps for most of his life.

Develop Tolerance of Others

The first step in socialization is related to the maxim we explored in Volume Two, Chapter 3, "Take what you can get closest to what you

SOCIALIZE

- Develop Tolerance of others.
  - Teach kindness.
  - Interact with others in non-task focused ways.
  - Allow people to adjust to their own personal space.
- Promote "Unconditional Positive Regard."
  - Provide attention and praise for each person's interests and gifts.
  - Facilitate occasions for successful interaction.
- Introduce giving and receiving.
  - Encourage people to give and do for others.
  - Promote expressions of appreciation.

want." This process follows the classical conditioning paradigm for developing a person's tolerance for social interaction. We let the person with the defensive style know that she is in control of the level of interaction, but we keep assisting her in getting a little closer to the desired outcome (social interaction) with each engagement. We do this with the conviction that wanting to be by herself is in the same class as wanting her Little Mermaid coloring book. It is a lifestyle based on incomplete information and experience. We firmly believe that when someone learns the joys of social interaction, the opportunities that come with the development of relationships, they will likely choose to be social, at least to some degree. Our task is to gradually introduce the defensive person, the person who rejects social relationships, to the joys of inclusion.

Self-isolation and rejection of social relationships is often the result of an institutional emphasis on task focus, or a life where the *relationship experience* is punitive and/or painful. When the level of engagement is low, when supported routines are lacking, when there are not enough staff to interact with everyone, the interactions that do occur usually involve tasks to be completed or that fit into the staff schedule or routines. Thus, the person who has lived in an institutional environment may think that the only time someone interacts with her is to try to get her to do something, or to "mess with" her. One thing we can do to help someone develop a tolerance of other people is to relate to them in other than task-focused ways.

Promote Unconditional Positive Regard

One way to diminish task focus flies in the face of the *do to* style of training that uses all desired items and events as reinforcers, things that are only received contingent on the presence of a particular target behavior. Socialization is one area in which the strict management of contingencies may be inappropriate. When we are helping a person who has been deprived of life experiences to mend, we must emphasize unconditional positive regard for that person. People in Groups I (the Revered) and II (Us), [see Volume One, Chapter 1] often exhibit such regard, despite a person's challenging behavior. We call this courtesy or kindness. Expressions of kindness are the primary lubricant that keeps the wheels of community relationships rolling. Kindness should be modeled for people who may have little experience of being the recipients of it. And we must offer them opportunities to demonstrate attitudes of kindness.

Introduce Giving and Receiving

People with intellectual disabilities and other disabilities have been on the receiving end of giving far too long. They are commonly seen as needy and dependent, with nothing to give. How would that make you feel? Giving to others can be a key to building self-esteem, a capacity for kindness and caring, and relationships with others.

An excellent way of learning kindness is to volunteer to do some caring thing. Volunteering can also be an entree into community participation. A good example is the people requiring pervasive supports who volunteer once a week at the local Humane Society shelter. Doing some simple task for the animals gives people an opportunity to be successful in giving; and, it is sometimes a lot easier to show kindness toward orphaned animals than it is toward impatient store managers.

Even if all a person can do is hold the kittens for a few minutes, this simple act encompasses integration, participation and relationships. A person who successfully helps out on this level may meet someone (another volunteer) who will issue an invitation to join in the next Humane Society walk-a-thon. Participating in the walk-a-thon earns the walker (or wheeler) a T-shirt, which proclaims, "I am somebody. I have something to give."

Often people who have been labeled Outsiders do not receive appreciation because they don't know how to offer it. Our task becomes that of showing people how to say thank you, write a note of appreciation, or give a gift in return for a favor. Expressing appreciation to others makes you a more attractive person. It is an important element of socialization.

Socialization is a process of becoming socially and emotionally acclimated to a new environment. It could almost be called decompression or resensitization. If we are to help people make the journey from exclusion to inclusion, we must support them along the way with patience, understanding and imagination.

We start with what the person can tolerate, then help them open their world, opportunity by opportunity.

Connect

The previous chapter explored the three building blocks of Universal Enhancement–integration, participation and relationships. People who have been Outsiders for some time often lose the ties that bind them with people and places in their home communities. On many of the functional assessments of people coming out of institutional placements, we read such things as, "Does not bond with others" or "Avoids relationships." We now approach relationship building as one of the tools of Universal Enhancement–connection.

Connection is sometimes known, in psychological circles, as reciprocal bonding, a fancy name for "becoming friends." A psychologist with whom I worked has come up with an operant definition of bonding.

Toolbox

An Operant Definition of Bonding

May occur at one, or all of three levels, and may be reciprocal.

- Level One: One person becomes a signal for the availability of reinforcement of another (Discriminative Stimulus Function).
- Level Two: One person becomes a reinforcer for another in regard to specific situations/context and specific behavior (Acquired Reinforcer Value).
- Level Three: One person becomes a reinforcer for another in a generalized fashion across situations, and in regard to a variety of behaviors (Generalized Reinforcer Value).

Ideally, bonding will be bilateral and occurs at Level Three. It may, unfortunately, grow slowly through contact, be unilateral and progress.

William R. McCuller, PhD[5]

This elegant precision of a psychological definition by Dr. McCuller is another way of describing the process of developing a relationship.

Level One: What you do to/for me

Level One occurs when the person with whom you are bonding knows that you have access to something she wants. Even a cat, not renowned for their bonding abilities, can manage a relationship at this level. If you are the person with the can opener or the one who opens the front door, you're the cat's friend. There is a bond, but it's not personal. The neighbor who comes in to your home to feed the cat when you are away will also be the object of the bond–if she has the can opener.

5 From conversations with Dr. William R. McCuller, Ph.D., circa June, 1995.

CONNECT

Nurture the establishment of friendships.

- Provide opportunity for interacting with individuals who are not paid to interact, not family members and who do not have disabilities.
- Recognize that developing a friendship takes time. Don't rush it.

Foster mutual smiles and touches.

- Demonstrate your connections with others through appropriate smiles and touches.

Promote a sense of humor.

- Have a good time: share laughter and the comic moments of life.

Celebrate special events, life's accomplishments and being together.

Many Level One relationships exist in institutional settings. When relationships are based on who has what and how can I get it (what we might call politics), Level One is about as far as a person can go. Thus, the nurse with the nasty tasting medicine is avoided and the man with the key to the dining room is a friend.

It is interesting to note that some studies of the ways in which people in institutional settings form relationships indicate that many such people view all of their relationships as intimate. Having had no experience of the range of closeness most of us have, from casual acquaintances to intimate lovers, people deprived of relationship opportunities are fooled into thinking that staff are their best friends.

Level Two: Relating to familiar people

Level Two is a little more sophisticated. The bond is based not on the receipt of a specific reward but on a connection that has been made within a certain specific context.

When I am out walking at the local park, there is a woman who always says hello and makes a friendly comment about the weather or about how good it is to be walking. I do not know her name or anything else about her. What we share is a common context–walking at the track. The bond is such that I look forward to exchanging greetings with her when I see her approaching. This is the kind of bond we see in young children. We say, "She responds to familiar people." The message is, "I know you. You're supposed to be here. I feel comfortable when you are around."

It is possible to have Level Two relationships in institutional settings. One common developmental milestone is "Responds to familiar people." Given the existence of paid staff who appear at time intervals (shifts), scheduled routines for daily living events, and assigned tasks to particular people, Level Two bonding is quite common. Those of us who have worked in settings that keep relationships on this level may have come to accept, and even desire them. I feel good when a person to whom I offer supports and assistance recognizes me. But how often are these relationships continued outside of the work setting? How many of us have "residents" sharing our Thanksgiving table, unless it is our scheduled day to work?

Level Three: Having a friend

Level Three is what we commonly describe as friendship. We like to be with the other person in a wide variety of situations, engaging in lots of different behaviors. We have come to know and care about another person. The bond is bilateral, that is, the feeling is mutual.

How does this development come about? Dr. McCuller suggests that it may grow slowly, from only one of the participants. Or it may occur immediately, like falling in love. The hope is that bonding will occur, and the task is to help people who have had little experience of or opportunity for friendship to develop their capacity to form bonds.

Ralph Waldo Emerson wrote, "The only way to have a friend is to be one." (Essays: First Series [1841] Friendship)[6] How, then, is someone going to have a friend who doesn't know how to be a friend? The

[6] Ralph Waldo Emerson, *Friendship*, in *Selected Essays* (Chicago: Book Production Industries, Inc., 1959).

answer is that they'll have to learn. Knowing how to be a friend, how to greet someone, how to respond to their overtures, how to ask someone to dinner, how to send flowers to their hospital bed or a card on their birthday–these are skills we all had to learn. Unfortunately, they are not often the kinds of skills that show up in the usual planning process for the people to whom we supply services and supports. In fact, we have sometimes been guilty of teaching staff to keep their distance, in order to establish a therapeutic relationship.

More creative and challenging than this process of maintaining professional distance would be an admonition that each of us should model the skills of bonding. We need to give smiles and hugs, not just as reinforcers, but as the building blocks of relationships. We need to be able to go up to someone who requires pervasive supports, give him a hug, and say, "I like you. You're a good guy," non-contingently, just because he is a good and valuable person.

We need to learn to promote a sense of humor in the people to whom we provide supports. It's okay to laugh, tell a joke and share the comic moments of life. Humor breaks down barriers and builds up relationships. And people with a sense of humor are more attractive than people who are dour and reserved.

Bonding

In order to have a friend - You must be one

Finally, we must celebrate life's special events together. Few activities do more to cement the bonding of relationships than the sharing of accomplishments and personal milestones. We can have a housewarming party (not an agency open house) to celebrate a person's new residence. We can have a party at a nearby pizza restaurant to celebrate a man's first paycheck. We can attend funerals, weddings, and baby showers with the people we support. Participation in the activities of relating is the only way relationships can be formed.

Connections take time. We'll have to "fake it 'til we make it." We'll have to take what we can get closest to what we want. We'll have to work on mending and socialization and communication. We'll have to share our feelings and demonstrate caring. The result is worth the effort. Emerson added, later in his essay on friendship, "A friend may well be reckoned the masterpiece of Nature."7

Communicate

Another way of supporting people in attaining the essence of a relationship is communication. Often, those of us who work with people who have limited communication skills are still stuck in the Developmental Model of communication. We want to communicate with them on their level, so we talk with them in the simplistic way we would talk with a child, starting with simple words and only later, when we think they have made progress, expanding into sentences. But such limits on our communication impose limits on our respect for the other person, as well. We place a barrier between ourselves and another person if we are not willing to communicate with them the way we communicate with our family and friends.

We may find ourselves saying of a person who speaks no words, "She has no communication skills." Then, at the same planning meeting, we might be discussing how to respond to her "tantrums," during which she rips her clothes and breaks furniture. Do we not realize that this

7 Ralph Waldo Emerson, *Friendship*, in *Selected Essays* (Chicago: Book Production Industries, Inc., 1959).

"behavior" is a bold effort to communicate her needs? Maybe she's unhappy because a friend snubbed her at work today. Maybe her ear hurts because of an infection. Maybe she feels powerless to affect a rigid schedule. Maybe she just doesn't like the color of the curtains or the style of the furniture! Simply stated, *Anger communicates unmet needs. LISTEN!* Many of the challenging behaviors we see are often due to the frustration a person with communication difficulties feels when they are not listened to. Exercising the skills of active listening, paying close attention, and not being too quick to say our own piece, will go a long way toward accomplishing our goals of Socialization and Connection.

MAXIM: *Anger communicates unmet needs. LISTEN!*

Being able to communicate affect, how a person feels, is too often not addressed when picture/symbol boards, manual signs, communication wallets, and voice synthesizers are used as supports in expressive communication. These devices and procedures may help a person ask for more milk or tell us that he needs to use the bathroom. Being able to do these things does bring improvements in the person's quality of life, but how do we support being able to say, "I'm sad because my friend is away on vacation" or "I love you"?

"Violence is the language of the unheard." *-- Dr. Martin Luther King, Jr.*

Active Listening

Square off
Open
Leaning
Eye contact
Reflecting

MAXIM: *Violence is the language of the unheard. –Rev. Martin Luther King, Jr.*

People learn how to express anger or sadness or happiness not by learning new words but by seeing others express their feelings. What if you lived in a place where no one ever laughed or told a joke? Or the only tears you ever saw were tears of rage and pain? Share your feelings with people who you serve and support. Reciprocate when they smile. You might be amazed at the responsiveness they can demonstrate in return and how expressive they can be of their own feelings, when they know someone will take the time and make the effort to listen.

TALE

Sharing Pete's Death

When I arrived for work at Charlie's home, he could see that there was something bothering me. I usually come in with a smile and ask Charlie about his day at the workshop. Today, I just didn't feel like doing that.

Charlie doesn't speak, but he came up to me and put his hand on my arm, looking into my face as if to ask, "What's wrong?" I tried to cover with a feeble smile, but a tear came out instead.

"I'm sorry, Charlie," I said. "I'm feeling kind of blue this afternoon. You see, this morning, I had to take my old dog, Pete, to the vet's and have him put to sleep."

My voice cracked as I related to Charlie the harrowing events of the morning–the difficult decision, followed by the actual death itself, as I held my old friend in my arms. When I looked up from my narrative, there was a tear in Charlie's eye, too. Then he tugged on my sleeve, his indication that he wanted me to go somewhere with him.

I followed Charlie into his bedroom, where he began rummaging through a dresser drawer. Suddenly, he plucked an old, bent photo from the jumble of saved objects and junk that made up his "collections" drawer. He showed it to me. It was a photo of Charlie, squatting down to pet old Pete. It had been taken last summer at our picnic in the mountains.

I sat on Charlie's bed with him, and we both had a good cry. We will both miss Pete, but we will take comfort in the bond that has grown between us through sharing our common loss.

COMMUNICATE

Exercise skills of listening.

- Role model listening to others.
- Listen slowly and carefully.

Share expressions of feelings.

- Share your feelings - show your emotional side.

Support self-determination and self-advocacy.

- Allow individuals to exercise control over their lives.
- Recognize that skills acquisition enhances self-determination.

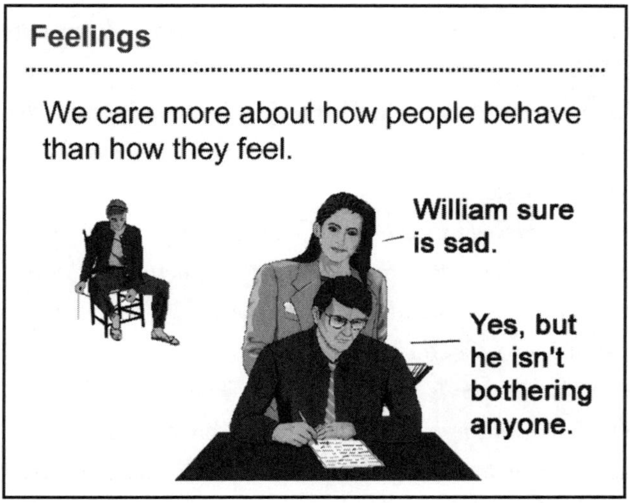

MAXIM: *Share your feelings.*

Initiate

The word "initiate" has some marvelous dictionary definitions that contribute significantly to our understanding of the concept.

To cause to begin

The first definition is "to cause to begin." When we assist people who require extensive support, particularly if they have spent a portion of their lives in places that manifest many of the institutional characteristics, the thing we are causing to begin is a life. Yes, a life. We are called upon to provide the opportunities and supports the person needs to build a meaningful life, filled with cherished persons, important rituals, significant events.

People who are just now getting the opportunity to live among us cannot build a life around learning to put on underarm deodorant; that's not where it's at. It is not necessary to begin with childish skills in order to make a beginning. We must begin with the things that are important to the person we are supporting and assisting.

To introduce

The second dictionary meaning of initiate is "to introduce (a person) to a new field, interest, skill, or activity." We introduce the person to choice-making; relationship building; having stories to tell of activities in which they've been an active participant; telling others about skills they're proud of. There is such a wonderful range of activities and attitudes and experiences that make up the quality of a life. We have the opportunity, the honor, to be the key that unlocks access to things a person may never have experienced before. What a shame it would be if we forfeited that opportunity because the person to whom we were providing support had yet to pass his "appropriate social greetings" program.

MAXIM: *You do not have to prove yourself to have a reasonable life. –Todd Risley, Ph.D.*

Introductions are an important part of our new role as community access worker, the guide who helps a person get past the Gatekeepers and barriers that are scattered through the community. When we are out and about (participating) with the person we are assisting, we must look for opportunities to introduce her to friends, neighbors, business people, mer-

INITIATE

- **Build upon the activities and items valued by the person– individualize.**
  - **Identify strengths – they form the basis of future growth.**
- **Promote rituals of membership.**
  - **Encourage participation in activities that say "I belong."**
  - **Celebrate the milestones of developing a presence.**
- **Introduce.**
  - **Seize upon all opportunities to assist others in making new acquaintances.**
- **Assure that the skills acquired enhance the quality of the person's life.**

chants. When we walk into the greeting card shop with Edgar and we see our friend Ethel, we can say, "Hi, Ethel. I'd like you to meet Edgar. He's new to the community, and I'm helping him find his way around."

Ethel might then turn from the card rack and say, "Pleased to meet you, Edgar," and shake his hand.

Edgar may need a little prompting or assistance to follow through with the next step in this little conversational gambit, but that's our job.

Now that introductions have been made, we can become engaged in a conversation with Ethel, learning that she is seeking a card for Walter, the grocery store produce manager. Tomorrow is Walter's birthday. Edgar now realizes that he knows Walter (he helped Edgar weigh the potatoes yesterday), and he would like to get Walter a birthday card, too.

To admit into membership

The third definition of initiate gives us a glimpse of the mystery, profundity, and depth of what we have set about to do. It says that to initiate is "to admit into membership, as with ceremonies or ritual." This brings us back to Volume Two, Chapter 2, where habilitation was defined as imparting the skills one needed "to qualify."

People who are new to our communities, who have spent years away in some institutional setting, are like new immigrants to our country. They may not know the language, the customs, how to get around or do business. They have been excluded from membership in our society. They often have no network of supportive relationships and no points of access from which to develop one. They have few stories to tell about themselves or their experiences. They may have nothing to celebrate and very little to share. In our initiation strategies, we must help these newcomers become full members, with us, of our cities, towns, churches, workplaces.

Some appropriate initiatory activities are:

- Obtaining a state-issued photo ID card from the driver's license bureau (even if the person does not have the skills to drive), thus becoming a "card carrying" member of the community
- Registering to vote, thus being "on the list" of people who count

Pathway to Friendship

Every relationship/friendship one forms in their life, other than with family, is developed as a result of playing (participating) an active role. The relationships/ friends that one has nurtured as a(n):

Parishioner who collected the tithe at church...

Camper who won first place in diving at the Girl/Boy Scout Camp...

Employee who brought tomatoes to work from the garden...

Patient who consoled their roommate at the hospital...

Volunteer who raised funds for a worthy cause...

Member who ran for office in a social club...

Pathway to Friendship, cont.

Neighbor who lent their garden tools...

Athlete who played shortstop on a softball team...

Student who played high school band...

Prisoner who served time following a conviction for tax evasion...

Parent who volunteered time at their child's school as a room monitor...

Gambler who served as the "bank" in a weekly poker game...

...Enhances the quality of one's life.

People who lack friends tend to lack roles.

• Getting a job, whether paid or volunteer, becoming someone who "makes a contribution"

• Joining a Neighborhood Watch organization, thus becoming a person who cares about his neighbors.

We must be creative in helping people find ways of belonging. With Universal Enhancement, everyone, every human being on this planet, is already, right now, qualified to be a full, participating member of the human race, with all the rights and privileges that entails. If one of our fellow humans has not been admitted to membership, has been seen as not qualifying, it is our task to design and initiate the appropriate ceremonies or rituals to say, "Welcome. You're one of us."

Toolbox

Universal Enhancement Checklist

The following checklist can help you assess the extent to which the important processes of Universal Enhancement are occurring in any setting. Give each item a score from 0-10. A 0 indicates the complete absence of the condition. A score of 5 would mean the glass is half full. A 10 is full realization of that particular aspect.

Mend	
Are obstacles in people's lives identified?	
Does the environment include modifications to hurdle those obstacles?	
Do all staff participate in designing creative Life Stiles to support people in overcoming barriers to a full life?	
Is gentle physical support used to redirect challenging behaviors and protect from injury?	
Is choice-making supported as an option to challenging behavior?	
Are Temporary Medication Plans based on adequate assessment and regular review?	
Are new medication doses started low and increased slowly as the need arises?	
SUBTOTAL	

Socialize Is tolerance of others modeled and encouraged?	
Are staff teaching kindness and caring through role modeling?	
Are people interacting with others in a way that is not task-focused?	
Are people allowed to adjust to their own personal space?	
Is attention and praise provided for everyone's interests and gifts?	
Are occasions provided for successful interaction?	
Are people encouraged to give and do for others?	
Are expressions of appreciation promoted?	
SUBTOTAL	
Connect Is the establishment of friendships nurtured?	
Are opportunities provided for interacting with individuals who are not paid to interact, not family members, and who do not have disabilities?	
Do staff recognize that friendship takes time and should not be rushed?	
Are connections with others modeled through appropriate smiles and touches?	
Is a sense of humor promoted?	
Are good times shared, including the comic moments of life?	
Are celebrations included such as special events, life's accomplishments, and being together?	
SUBTOTAL	

Communicate	
Do staff understand and exercise the skills of listening?	
Is listening to others modeled and reinforced?	
Do staff listen slowly and carefully?	
Do people share expressions of feeling?	
Do staff model the sharing of feeling and revealing their emotional sides?	
Is self-determination and self-advocacy supported in observable, concrete ways?	
Are people encouraged to exercise control over their own lives?	
Can staff point to ways they demonstrate how skill acquisition enhances self-determination?	
SUBTOTAL	
Initiate	
Are staff aware of individual preferences, and do they individualize activities to build on people's strengths?	
Are individual strengths (as well as deficits) identified?	
Do new staff and new residents participate in rituals of membership?	
Does everyone have the opportunity to participate in activities that say, I belong?	
Are the milestones of developing a Presence (achievements, memberships, new relationships) celebrated?	
Do staff look for opportunities to make introductions?	
Is the formation of relationships that can become natural supports encouraged and achieved?	
SUBTOTAL	
GRAND TOTAL	

Scores

Perfect score is 380.

0-150:	Is this an institution?
151-250:	Some old paradigms are still at work here.
251-300:	There's a new day dawning!
301-380:	Universal Enhancement is making everyone's life better. Celebrate!

3

Having a Life... and Beyond

It is with some hesitation and a good deal of humility that I propose another approach to supporting individuals with disabilities and other Outsiders.

I have experienced and been affected by many changes in 30 some years of working to provide needed supports and services to all kinds of people whose conditions or circumstances have caused them to be cast aside. I have seen, and even been a part of, ways of behaving toward Outsiders that were excluding, demeaning and dehumanizing. I have met each new guiding philosophy for the services we deliver with the joy and exhilaration that come from discovering a better way of doing a job I care very much about. I have worked under the Medical/Custodial Model; I was a caretaker beholden to doctors and nurses for the ways I perceived and related to patients.

I was excited about the possibilities of the Developmental Model, and I strove mightily to help people move up on those developmental data document graphs. I saw incredible change driven by the principles of the Habilitation Model, as the ICF-MR regulations drove agencies to some semblance of normalization.

I advocated and propagated each new approach. But I was always willing to leave each adopted philosophy behind, eager to move forward and embrace a better way.

I have never before been as enthusiastic about the promises held out for a new way of looking at our work as I am at the prospects of Universal Enhancement. I see it as a way of keeping the excitement in our work. I teach, coach, and consult the content and principles of Universal Enhancement daily and I am frequently asked how I maintain my enthusiasm. Those who are not yet believers and the uninitiated will soon grow to learn that Universal Enhancement inspires those who embrace it in being motivated to achieve the vision. It is exciting. It is that kind of energy, an enthusiasm that lights our way through years of hard work, that Universal Enhancement can bring to those of us who work in the field of human services.

But is Universal Enhancement just another step along this long and sometimes tedious road? Will I be back in a few years, discussing and writing about how I used to believe in Universal Enhancement, but now I've gone beyond that to... whatever? It is possible. I hope I'll be open enough to new thinking that I can see and accept another better way when I find it or it finds us.

There are several significant ways in which Universal Enhancement differs from the other models. That is because it is not really a model at all. Universal Enhancement is not some kind of static belief, a school of thought that has dogmas and creeds that must be observed. It is, rather, an ongoing process that changes all the time; it is synergistic, organic and holistic. It applies the same kinds of ever-changing, inconsistent, growth-producing principles to the lives of Outsiders that most of us take for granted in our own lives. It is not a template or standard that can be used to judge whether or not people have reached some imagined goal. It allows for failures as well as successes; solitude as well as intimacy; dejection as well as elation.

There is no down side to Universal Enhancement. It is not a new technology, born in the halls of academe, that has to be tested or proven. It is not some fantasy of social engineering, a give-away program that will bankrupt the nation. It violates no standards or regulations. It poses no ethical dilemmas or harmful side effects. There is, quite simply, no reason not to follow the course of Universal Enhancement.

Why Should it Be Any Different?

The two principal differences between Universal Enhancement and all earlier models of service are that Universal Enhancement: 1) provides assurances that the person who needs support and assistance is the one who makes the decisions about how, where, and by whom those supports and assistance are provided; and 2) removes the social barriers that segregate people who have been treated as Outsiders as a result of their disabilities or other personal characteristics. These differences are the essence of the critical paradigm shift that is sweeping the field of human services.

If you have viewed people who are different from Normatives as them, as people who need their own kind of life that is radically different from the life you want for yourself, Universal Enhancement requires nothing short of a conversion experience. In the same way that people can be suddenly struck by a spiritual awakening, the focus of Universal Enhancement makes the world appear a different place. Once you see it, it is so obvious you wonder how you could have missed it. The shift is like those 3-D pictures that look, at first, like nothing but splotches of color. Once the image comes into focus, you have difficulty not seeing it.

One of the working titles for this book was "Why Should It Be Any Different?" Asking that question helps us see that the essence of Universal Enhancement is that we stop thinking of people who are over 65 years old or who have mental illness or who have physical disabilities or intellectual disabilities as being essentially different from us. Instead of asking, What do they want? or What do they need? we begin to ask, What does Harriet want? or What does Raymond need?

But of whom do we ask those questions? This is the final step, the piece that breaks down the differences. We ask Harriet and Raymond. We can no longer afford the luxury of believing that just because we are professionals or family members or authorities of some kind, we know better than Harriet or Raymond what they want and need out of life.

Equally important is that we begin to empathize with people who are Outsiders. No longer seeing them as wholly alien, we can ask, What would I want if I were in their shoes? That is the standard we must use–Is this what I would want for my life? We can no longer be experts doing to, or caretakers doing for. We must see ourselves as supports, working side by side with the people to whom we provide support, even staying in the background when necessary, for that is probably how we would like to be treated, were our status exchanged for theirs. We must do with.

MAXIM: *Do not treat others the way you would wish to be treated; but rather treat others the way you would treat yourself under the most challenging of circumstances.*

Relationships

We emphasize relationships, not only for the sake of the person who needs supports but also, and perhaps more importantly, for our own sake. For it is relationship that makes everyone's life more worthwhile.

According to Karl Menninger, "The establishment or re-establishment of relationship with fellow human beings is the basic architecture of normal life... To live, we say, is to love, and vice versa."[8]

If *relationship* does, indeed, form the basic architecture of normal life, then it is there we need to build. We must leave our training structures behind and harken to the structures of the human heart and spirit.

Fulfillment of the Promise

Universal Enhancement is for everybody. That's what makes it universal. Universal Enhancement will be realized when we no longer define a quality life in terms of treatment teams and program plans, schedules and menus. When we seek to remove the barriers that cause handicaps and stop segregating people on the basis of their abilities, Universal Enhancement will become a reality.

The fulfillment of the promise of Universal Enhancement does not

[8] Karl Menninger, *The Vital Balance: The Life Process in Mental Illness* (New York: Viking Press, 1963) 294.

depend on the professional community adopting new assessment devices or training techniques. Rather, and most importantly, it requires the efforts of good men and women everywhere who will see people as people and treat them as neighbors. Indeed, we can be, should be, midwives only, helping during the transition from the old ways to the new.

Universal Enhancement will have happened when we who work as professionals in the field of services to Outsiders will be out of a job, when families and friends and co-workers and choir members and grocery store employees will give support and assistance to everyone who needs it.

Universal Enhancement will come to fruition when everyone, regardless of how they look or how smart they are or how many things they have difficulty doing, will be treated with dignity and respect and appreciation by all.

About the Author

Thomas E. Pomeranz, Ed.D. is a nationally recognized authority, clinician and consultant in the field of developmental disabilities. Over the last 30 years, Dr. Pomeranz has conducted hundreds of seminars and programs throughout the United States and Canada. He was the keynote presenter at the Fifth International Conference on Developmental Disabilities and Aging in Cyprus, Greece. Additionally, Dr. Pomeranz is noted for his innovative approach to leadership and management training.

Dr. Pomeranz holds bachelor and master of science degrees in education and mental retardation from Indiana University, and has done post-graduate work in experimental psychology at Notre Dame University. He received his doctorate from Indiana University with a concentration in mental health administration. Dr. Pomeranz has held top-level positions in three large state-operated facilities as well as community-based service organizations. Throughout his career, Dr. Pomeranz has held faculty posts in several universities and is currently an adjunct faculty member of Saint Louis University's School of Public Health.

Dr. Pomeranz is the principal consultant of ResCare Training Technologies, the external training and consulting business of ResCare, the nation's largest provider of services for people with developmental disabilities.

A Note on the Type

The text of this book was set in Electra, a typeface designed in 1935 by the renowned designer and illustrator William A. Dwiggins (1880-1956). A standard book typeface since its release due to the evenness of design and high legibility, this face cannot be classified as either modern or old style. It is not based on any historical model, nor does it echo any particular period or style. It avoids the extreme contrasts between thick and thin elements that mark most modern faces, and it gives a feeling of fluidity, warmth, personality, and speed.

Printed and bound by McNaughton & Gunn Inc.,
Saline, Michigan

Book design by Diane J. Bell
Cover illustration by Rob Colvin
The artwork in this book is a compilation of clip art and original drawings.
The original drawings are by various artists, none of whom expect to receive credit, except where indicated in the image.